UNITED STATES MILI

IN THE

AH-64 APACHE

Gareth Stevens PUBLISHING

Thomas Kingsley Troupe

Please visit our website, www.garethstevens.com. For a free color catalog of all our high-quality books, call toll free 1-800-542-2595 or fax 1-877-542-2596

Cataloging-in-Publication Data

Names: Troupe, Thomas Kingsley.
Title: AH-64 Apache / Thomas Kingsley Troupe.
Description: Buffalo, NY : Gareth Stevens Publishing, 2027. | Series: United States military might: in the air | Includes glossary and index.
Identifiers: ISBN 9781482480726 (pbk.) | ISBN 9781482480733 (library bound) | ISBN 9781482480740 (ebook)
Subjects: LCSH: Apache (Attack helicopter)--Juvenile literature. | Attack helicopters--United States--Juvenile literature.
Classification: LCC UG1232.A88 T768 2027 | DDC 623.7463--dc23

First Edition

Published in 2027 by
Gareth Stevens Publishing
2544 Clinton Street
Buffalo, NY 14224

Designer: Kathy Walsh/Beeline Media and Design, Inc.
Editor: Tricia Hoffman

Photo credits: Cover, pp. 1 Rawpixel.com, Flow37 (Swirl Background), Anna Lysohor (Bottom Bars), Kavya/Shutterstock.com; p 4 Christopher Freeman/Public Domain; p 4 Sgt. James Larimer/Public Domain; p 6 & 8 Sgt Olivia Cowart/Public Domain; p 10 thomas Alvarez/Public Domain; p 11 Sgt 1st Class Kris Bonet/Public Domain; p 11 Everett Collection/Shutterstock.com; p 12 Joseph Kumzak/Public Domain; p 13 Sgt Olivia Cowart/Public Domain; p 14 VanderWolf Images/Shutterstock.com; p 16 Courtesy Photo/Public Domain; p 17 Capt. Daniel Andrews/Public Domain; p 18 Staff Sgt Randis Monroe/Public Domain; p 19 Sgt Charlie Duke/Public Domain; p 20 Lt Col Robert Fellingham/Public Domain; p 21 Phoenix Pixels/Shutterstock.com; p 22 Sgt Charlie Duke/Public Domain; p 23 Robert Harnden/Public Domain; p 24 Sgt Michael Majors/Public Domain; p 26 Sgt Mitchell Johnson/Public Domain; p 28 Spc. John Farmer/Public Domain

Printed in China

CPSIA compliance information: Batch #QS27GS: For further information contact Gareth Stevens, New York, New York at 1-800-542-2595.

TABLE OF CONTENTS

CHAPTER 1

ARMORED AIR ATTACK

Dust kicks up and blows across the desert. U.S. Army trucks and tanks rumble by. They are headed back to base after a **reconnaissance** mission. Above them, a U.S. helicopter flies. The giant **rotor** blades are a blur, spinning above the aircraft.

The U.S. pilots aboard the helicopter are keeping watch. They're in dangerous territory. The co-pilot in the front seat

sees something. He sees movement in his helmet's display screen. There could be trouble. The U.S. copilot lets the pilot know. They fly ahead of the Army tanks.

The helicopter roars across the desert. It slows as it gets closer to a series of large rock formations. It **hovers** for a while, scanning the area. Something was there just a moment ago. The pilot sweeps around for a better look. Hiding behind the rocks is a group of enemy soldiers. They turn and aim their rocket launcher at the helicopter. What will happen next?

The AH-64 Apache is one of the deadliest helicopters in the world. It can move quick and fly low. It's loaded with an arsenal of awesome weapons. It's the Army's guardian in the sky. The AH-64 is an incredible helicopter!

CHAPTER 2

EAGLE EYE IN THE SKY

The AH-64 Apache is an attack helicopter. The A in its name stands for "attack." The H stands for "helicopter."

The Apache is built for battle! The AH-64 has twin engines. If one fails or is damaged, the other can keep it airborne.

The AH-64 has a unique cockpit. The pilot sits behind the co-pilot. She flies the helicopter and is in charge of navigation. The co-pilot sits in the front seat. He spots targets and controls the weapons. Both sections of the cockpit have flight and weapon controls. Either can take over the other's job if necessary!

The nose of the AH-64 is packed with technology. On its end is a system known as TADS. That stands for Target Acquisition and Designation System. It has an **infrared** scanner that helps find and track targets to attack.

Like all helicopters, the AH-64 has a main rotor above the **fuselage**. The four rotor blades spin fast, allowing for quick takeoff. There is also a tail rotor. It keeps the helicopter **stabilized**.

Apache warrior Geronimo

Native Namesake

The AH-64 Apache got its name from an American Indian tribe. Apache warriors were known for being smart and tough on the battlefield. The U.S. military wanted to honor the tribe. They gave it the "Apache" name in 1981.

The AH-64 has short wings on each side of the fuselage. They are used primarily for holding the helicopter's weapons. Various rocket pods and missiles can be attached to the wings. To make transporting the AH-64 easier, the wings and rotor blades can be detached.

Pilots inside the AH-64's cockpit are protected. The AH-64 is layered with reinforced armor. This protects them from enemy fire. Even the glass surrounding the cockpit is bulletproof!

CHAPTER 3

ALL-WEATHER AIRBORNE ASSAULT

The AH-1 Cobra attack helicopter had been in service since 1967. But the Army wanted something new.

In the early 1970s, the U.S. Army wanted a new attack helicopter. They wanted one that could protect ground troops and destroy tanks. It needed to be able to fly in any type of weather.

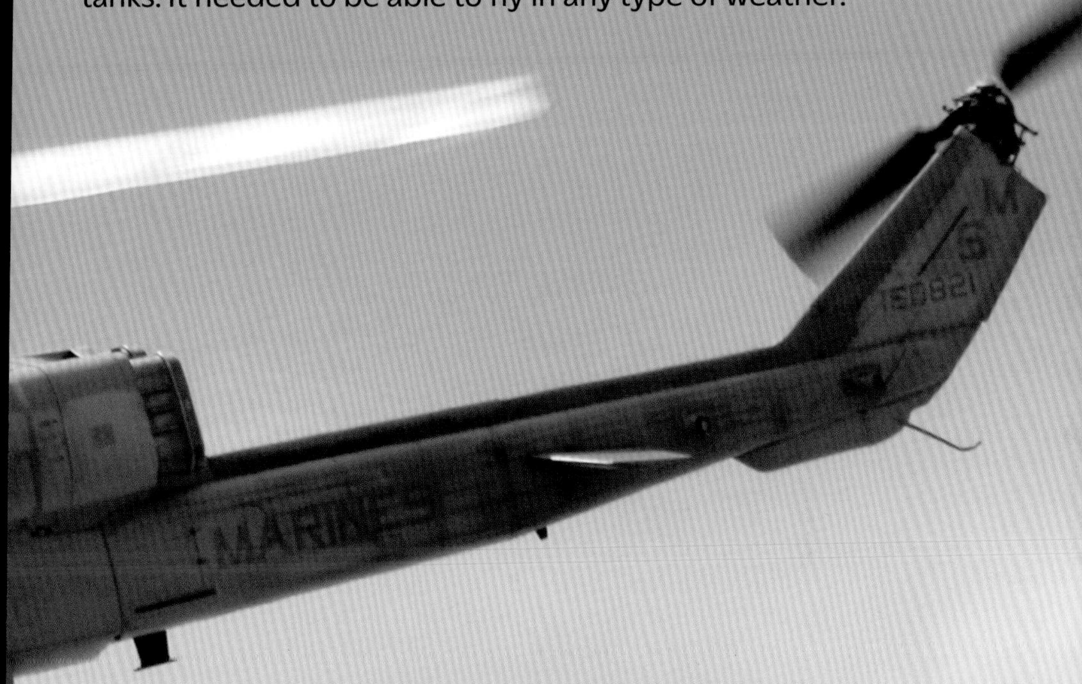

The Army started the Advanced Attack Helicopter, or AAH, program in 1972. Aeronautics engineers attempted to design the ultimate helicopter. During the development period, several companies came up with different concepts. They spent the next years working on getting the aircraft just right.

Hughes Helicopters and Bell made it to the final round of the AAH program. The military would decide which would win.

In September 1975, the Hughes YAH-64 **prototype** was flown. The next day, Bell demonstrated its helicopter. Both companies waited a full year for the Army's decision. But finally, Hughes Helicopters' design was chosen. In 1982, the AH-64 Apache was ready for service.

Night Vision

The AH-64 Apache was one of the first aircraft to use infrared night vision. That means it found targets by tracking their heat. It works in daytime or nighttime and through smoke!

CHAPTER 4

TOYS THAT MAKE NOISE

Many helicopters are mainly used to transport soldiers or supplies. But the AH-64 was made for battle! The AH-64 is built tough and brings a lot of weapons with it. It's like a flying tank!

The helicopter's radar sits above the rotor. The Longbow radar sends out invisible waves. It lets pilots know where enemies are. Some newer AH-64s have MUMT-X. It stands for Manned-Unmanned Teaming—Extended. It lets pilots send **drones** ahead into dangerous areas. The drones send back information about the enemy.

The AH-64 Apache can command drones like this one.

Underneath the fuselage is the M230 30mm chain gun. It's on a moveable turret. The gun can aim left and right. It can also tilt up and down. It can fire more than 600 rounds per second! The M230 works with the pilots' helmet. Where they look, the gun will aim!

Tucked under the AH-64's wings are the rest of the weapons systems. At the end of each wing are rocket launchers. They are cylinder-shaped with lots of holes in the front. Each hole is loaded with a rocket. Next to the rocket launchers are racks for missiles. Some of the missiles are known as "fire and forget." The co-pilot fires them but doesn't need to guide them to the target.

Apache vs. Godzilla

The AH-64 is famous. It has been in numerous TV shows, video games, and movies. It even fought Japan's giant-sized monster Godzilla in the 2014 movie!

CHAPTER 5

SKYBOUND STUDENTS

It takes a lot of training to fly an AH-64 Apache. Future pilots need to enlist in the Army to get started. After completing basic training, they'll eventually begin flight school. There, they'll practice flying smaller helicopters. They'll fly with instructors as co-pilots.

The extensive training takes place both in the air and on the ground. They'll fly larger, more powerful helicopters. They'll also spend time working in **simulators**. The AH-64 simulator is like an expensive video game. It's designed to function like a helicopter, without ever leaving the ground.

All of the courses and many simulator sessions take years to complete. Once done, the pilot is ready for the real thing. They start training in an AH-64. They will fly with instructors and other pilots. They'll learn both the pilot and co-pilot roles. They get hands-on training with the weapons systems.

After a few years of training, the pilot can fly AH-64 missions. They'll be assigned to a **squadron** or CAB. CAB stands for Combat Aviation Brigade. There, they will work with other pilots and members of the team. They'll get real-life experience flying the amazing Apache helicopter!

BRAVE
LIKE
BLYTHE

CHAPTER 6

MISSION ACCOMPLISHED!

When we last saw the AH-64 in action, enemy soldiers had aimed their rocket launcher at the helicopter. What will happen next?

A rocket fires. The U.S. pilot quickly veers to the left. The rocket swooshes past the AH-64, missing it completely. Ground forces fire machine guns at the helicopter. Its armor rattles with gunfire.

The pilot pulls the helicopter back as the co-pilot engages the chain gun. It syncs to his helmet and moves where he looks. As the AH-64 dodges another rocket attack, the co-pilot fires. Short bursts of bullets erupt from the gun. The threats are neutralized and the convoy is safe. Mission accomplished!

The AH-64 Apache is the deadliest helicopter in the sky. It's quick, tough, and loaded with weapons. It's the Army's aerial avenger that can square off against tanks! Its sensors and targeting system make it a fearsome foe. The AH-64 is a prime example of U.S. military might!

We Want One Too

The AH-64 isn't just used by the United States Army. Japan, Greece, South Korea, the United Kingdom, and more countries have purchased AH-64s for their militaries too.

A CLOSER LOOK

Reliable Rotors

The AH-64 Apache helicopter has been in service since 1984. The AH-64 has more than 5 million flight hours. It also has more than 1.3 million combat hours!

GLOSSARY

drones (DROHNZ): aircrafts with no humans on board that are controlled remotely

fuselage (FYOO-suh-lahzh): the main body of an aircraft where the passengers, crew, and cargo are carried

hovers (HUHV-urz): remains in one place in the air

infrared (in-fruh-RED): a kind of light that cannot be seen with the eyes

prototype (PROH-tuh-tipe): the first version of an invention that tests an idea to see if it will work

reconnaissance (ri-KAH-nuh-suhns): exploring and gathering information before a mission

rotor (ROH-tuhr): the part of a machine that turns or rotates

simulators (SIM-yuh-lay-turz): machines that allow you to experience or perform a complex task by imitating the conditions and controls

squadron (SKWAH-druhn): a group of ships, cavalry troops, or other military units

stabilized (STAY-buh-lized): firmly fixed; held steady

FACT CHECK

1. The AH in AH-64 Apache stands for ____.

   a. aerial/hovering   b. army/helmet   c. attack/helicopter

2. The Apache's prototype was first flown in _______.

   a. 1989   b. 1978   c. 1975

3. There are ____ seats in an AH-64 Apache helicopter.

   a. four   b. three   c. two

Answers: 1. c, 2. c, 3. c

FURTHER READING

Henzel, Cynthia Kennedy. *Powerful Military Aircraft*. The Child's World, 2024.

McKinney, Donna. *Apache Helicopter*. Bellwether Media, 2024.

ON THE INTERNET

Britannica Kids: Army

https://kids.britannica.com/kids/article/army/352785

Check out the basic functions of the U.S. Army and its ranks. You'll also get a peek into the military service's history.

Kiddle: McDonnell Douglas AH-64 Apache Facts for Kids

https://kids.kiddle.co/McDonnell_Douglas_AH-64_Apache

Get a bunch of facts and background about the unique AH-64 Apache. Learn about the different reasons the aircraft was created. There is also a collection of photos of the aircraft in action!

Publisher's note to educators and parents: Our editors have carefully reviewed these websites to ensure that they are suitable for students. Many websites change frequently, however, and we cannot guarantee that a site's future contents will continue to meet our high standards of quality and educational value. Be advised that students should be closely supervised whenever they access the internet.

INDEX

ABOUT THE AUTHOR

Thomas Kingsley Troupe is the author of a big ol' pile of books for kids. He's written about everything from ghosts to Bigfoot to third-grade werewolves. He even wrote a book about dirt. When he's not writing or reading, he gets plenty of exercise. Thomas had a really great GI Joe toy helicopter when he was younger. It looked a lot like the AH-64. It came with a pilot wearing a cowboy hat! Thomas lives in Woodbury, Minnesota, with his not-so-little offspring.